A McGRAW-HILL NEW BIOLOGY

Scientific Adviser: Dr. Gwynne Vevers
Curator of the Aquarium and Invertebrates,
The Zoological Society of London

PENGUINS

OTHER BOOKS IN THIS SERIES

A McGRAW-HILL NEW BIOLOGY

Bernard Stonehouse

Penguins

Illustrated by Trevor Boyer

McGRAW-HILL BOOK COMPANY

New York   St. Louis   San Francisco

Metric Conversion Table

1 centimeter (cm) = 0.39 inch
1 meter (m) = 3.27 feet
1 kilometer (km) = 0.62 mile

1 sq. centimeter = 0.15 sq. inch
1 sq. meter = 10.76 sq. feet
1 hectare = 2.47 acres
1 sq. kilometer = 0.39 sq. mile

1 kilogram (kg) = 2.21 lb. (avoirdupois)
1 tonne = 0.98 (long) ton

Library of Congress Cataloging in Publication Data

Stonehouse, Bernard.
  Penguins.

  (A McGraw-Hill new biology)
  Includes index.
  SUMMARY; Discusses several varieties of penguins,
their habitats, growth, and breeding habits.
    1. Penguins—Juvenile literature. [1. Penguins]
I. Boyer, Trevor. II. Title.
QL696.S473S76   598.4'41   79–13661
ISBN 0–07–061740–6

First distribution in the United States of America
by McGraw-Hill Book Company, 1979
Text © Bernard Stonehouse 1978
Illustrations © Trevor Boyer 1978
First printed in Great Britain for
The Bodley Head
by William Clowes (Beccles) Ltd., Beccles
First published 1978
Printed in Great Britain
123456789 7832109

Contents

Emperor

Chinstrap

Yellow-eyed

Peruvian

Erect-crested

Fairy

Six of the eighteen species of penguins. Emperors and Chin-straps are Antarctic species; Yellow-eyed Penguins live in New Zealand, and Peruvian Penguins in South America. Erect-crested Penguins breed on small islands to the south of New Zealand, while Fairy Penguins are found only in Australia and New Zealand.

1

Introducing penguins

Penguins are a family of seabirds, warm-blooded and feathered like all other birds, but flightless. Most birds need to fly, so that they can hunt widely for food and escape from enemies. Penguins walk, run and climb over rocks, but cannot fly at all. They are seen at their best in the sea, where they swim and dive with extraordinary skill. Of all the seabirds, they are the most expert in water. They "fly" through the water using their wings as flippers. Penguins spend much of their life at sea, returning to land only to breed and moult. But only their life on land has been observed and studied; how they live at sea still remains mostly a mystery.

The explorers who first saw penguins in the fifteenth and sixteenth centuries confused them with auks and guillemots, which are plentiful in northern oceans. Now we know they are not even related to these birds, though they may have originated from flying birds rather like them in the long distant past. Perhaps the penguin ancestors were auk-like birds that began to spend more time under water, diving deeper to catch their food below the levels where other seabirds fed. To dive well they would have had to grow bigger and heavier, and develop more plumage and fat to keep warm. They would have needed to lose the big wing feathers that once helped them to fly, but now slowed them down in the water. So they evolved the chunky body and flipper-wings and the distinctive penguin shape we know today.

All fossil remains of penguins have been found in the southern hemisphere, in Australia, New Zealand, South America, South Africa and Antarctica. These fragments of bone show that there have been penguins in the world for well over fifty million years. Some of the ancient penguins were much larger than any living today; the largest stood over 1.5 m tall and weighed about 130 kg. Giant penguins were swimming in the southern oceans long before whales and seals came on the scene. The last giant penguins died out about thirty million years ago.

200 cm

150 cm

100 cm

50 cm

0 cm

Relative sizes of some living and fossil penguins. Living species from left to right: Royal, Fairy, King, Emperor, Gentoo, Magellanic, Galapagos.

People who live in the northern hemisphere and see penguins only in zoos tend to think of them as rare birds, living entirely in the Antarctic. In fact, only a few kinds of penguins are rare and even fewer live in the polar regions; most are quite common birds of cool-temperate coasts, though only in the southern hemisphere. Rarest of all is the Galapagos Penguin, which lives on some of the Galapagos Islands off equatorial South America. Only three of the eighteen living species of penguins—Emperors, Adelies and Chinstraps—nest entirely among polar ice and snow. Most live on cool or temperate islands of the southern ocean—for example, South Georgia in the South Atlantic—where they nest among tussock grass or on rocky cliffs and headlands. Some live in wet coastal forests of New Zealand and South America, nesting among roots of trees and even roosting in the branches. Some species are sub-tropical or tropical, nesting in burrows on sandy desert shores. Penguins of warmer regions are mainly active at night, when the air is cooler and there are fewer people about to see them.

White-flippered Penguin, a mainly nocturnal species of New Zealand.

9

2

Penguins as birds

Penguins look quite different from all other birds. Their shape, the proportions of their body and their movements give them a rather human appearance, like fat, pompous old men. But these are all special adaptations for their unique way of life and make sense when you see penguins on their home ground, in or close to the sea.

The first and most striking difference is in the way they stand and walk. Most birds—gulls and ducks for instance—hold their body more or less horizontal on spindly legs, with their neck rising above in an S-curve. Penguins stand upright on short, stumpy legs, with neck and body in a straight line. The tail is usually a short prop trailing behind,

Adelie Penguin (left) and Brown Skua. The penguin's legs,
set far back along the body, are used for steering in
the water, and for standing upright on land.

with no obvious function but to be sat upon. Their upright stance causes them to walk with a roll; large penguins stroll, middle-sized ones waddle, and the smaller species tend to hop.

These penguin characteristics all arise from adaptations for life in water. Like whales, dolphins and seals, penguins need to be streamlined for swimming at speed. They stand upright because their legs are set far back along the body; this allows the feet to trail behind when the bird is swimming, well out of the way and causing the least possible drag. Feet and tail combine to form a compact steering rudder, which helps the bird to turn sharply in the water. The long neck darts out right and left to catch any fish or other prey swimming within reach. To support the weight of the body on land, the hips and lower spine are fused tightly together. With rigid hips and no waistline, penguins cannot bend in the middle, so the whole body sways at each step. Fast walking and running are difficult for them; if they need to move quickly, they fall forwards on to their breast feathers and toboggan, pushing themselves along with flippers and feet. They can toboggan faster than a person can run, especially over snow and ice.

Where most birds have large wings with flight feathers, penguins have narrow, thin flippers with feathers so small that they look like scales. Slender and firm like the blade of an oar, these propel the

King Penguin flipper (above) and gull wing (below).
Internal bony structure is similar in the two; the flipper
lacks the big flight feathers that allow the gull to fly,
but would be useless under water.

bird through the water at 25 km an hour or more. To
move the flippers rapidly against the water, penguins
have developed powerful breast muscles and strong
solid bones, which add much to their weight. Where
flying birds have to be as slender and lightweight
as possible, penguins can afford to be solid and
chunky; indeed being heavy and powerful may
help them to be more efficient at swimming and
diving. The smallest penguin, roughly as big as a
gull, is three to four times the weight of a gull. The
largest penguin in full fat can weigh up to 45 kg,
more than three times the weight of the heaviest
flying bird.

Some of a penguin's additional weight is made
up of insulation. Spending so much of their time
in cold water, penguins need dense plumage to keep

themselves waterproof and warm. Their feathers are shorter, more uniform and more tightly packed than those 'of other birds, with tips that overlap like tiles on a roof. Beneath the feathers is a layer of dense, woolly underdown, which acts as a kind of thermal underwear, and there is a thick layer of insulating fat under the skin. This insulation is so efficient that sometimes the penguins get too hot. To avoid overheating when ashore, especially when the sun shines strongly, a penguin can fluff up its feathers to let the warm air trapped close to its body escape. Sometimes they pant to cool off, or stand with flippers held out to catch a cooling breeze.

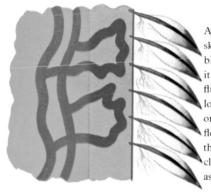 An overheated penguin's skin and blubber (left) has blood flowing freely through it, and the feathers are fluffed out so heat can be lost. A penguin in cold air or water (right) reduces the flow of blood in vessels of the skin and blubber, and closes its feathers to keep in as much heat as possible.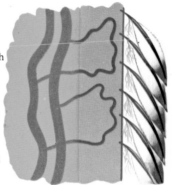

Penguins look fat because of the thickness of their feathers and blubber, and also because they have a big crop. This is necessary in a bird that feeds far from home, and that may have to carry food back for its young ones. The large bulk of big penguins helps them to dive deep; the largest penguins can dive to depths of well over 100 meters, and stay

Barbs inside the mouth help the penguin to catch and swallow slippery prey; Rockhopper Penguin.

under water for half an hour or more when searching for food. Most penguins eat fish, shrimp-like crustaceans or squid—all slippery creatures that are hard to catch and hold. Penguins have fleshy barbs on their tongue and the lining of their mouth, which point backwards down the throat and help them to hold their prey.

The eighteen different species of penguins range widely in size. The largest—the Emperor Penguin—stands over a meter tall and normally weighs about 30 kg. The smallest—the Fairy or Little Blue Penguin—is only 40 cm tall and barely weighs 1 kg. Most other penguins stand 40 to 60 cm and weigh 3 to 5 kg.

Most penguins are blue-black or blue-gray on

Extremes of size: it would take more than thirty Fairy
Penguins (left) to outweigh the one Emperor.

the back, and white in front, with very little other coloring except on the head and neck. This pattern too is an adaptation for swimming. In the water they appear dark above and pale below, making it difficult for seals and other enemies to spot them. The brilliant yellow crests that some species carry above their eyes, and the golden-yellow patches, white eye-rings, pink or orange bill plates and distinctive markings of other species show up clearly when the birds are swimming at the surface with their heads out of water; in this way they can identify each other on sight, and recognize birds of their own species.

But all penguins, big or small, have much in common—the same unique stance and rolling gait, the same plumpness and feathering, similar color patterns and the same miraculous efficiency as swimmers and divers. And they are all un-mistakably penguins.

3

Penguins of South Georgia

Penguins are widespread in the southern hemisphere, though most species live in the cooler waters of the southern ocean. Some of the largest penguin breeding colonies are found on islands south of latitude 50°S., where there are short, cool summers and long, very cold winters. The water is cold, seldom rising more than a few degrees above freezing point even in summer, but it is very rich in plant and animal life. Because food is so plentiful, many different kinds of seabirds breed on these remote southern islands, despite the snow, rain and blustering winds.

South Georgia, 2,000 kilometers east of Cape Horn, is just such an island. Four species of penguins breed there, three of them in large numbers. Largest and most colorful is the King Penguin, which lives on flat, muddy, tussock-covered ground close to sea level. There are seven or eight big colonies on the island, numbering thousands of pairs, and many much smaller colonies of a few dozen pairs. Gentoo Penguins, smaller and more plentiful than the King Penguins, also nest in the tussocks, often high on hillsides overlooking the sea. Their colonies usually contain a few hundred pairs but there are many more of them

◁King Penguins swimming at the surface, using their flippers as paddles, feet and tail as a rudder.

scattered along the coast in almost every bay and fjord. Macaroni Penguins nest mainly among rocks, in colonies of tens of thousands, on steep tumbling cliffs and rocky slopes close to the sea. They are seldom seen on beaches with the other penguins. A few hundred pairs of Chinstrap Penguins nest on South Georgia, but most Chin-straps breed farther south, on colder islands of the polar zone.

Chinstrap Penguin with young chicks.

Porpoising Gentoo Penguins.

In October, thousands of Gentoos return to the island, sleek and fat after their winter at sea. When they first return, the nest sites are still buried under thick snow, and the birds tend to stay on the beaches. But by late October the thaw has started, and the penguins move away from the sea to occupy their hillside colonies. Their trampling feet, helped by the warm sun and rain, make the snow melt rapidly. Within a few days the original nest sites—piles of stones, moss and old bones left from last year—reappear in the slushy, smelly mud.

Neither the wetness nor the strong smell seems to worry the penguins. As each site appears, one of the group moves in and reclaims it. This is usually a male, often the male of the pair that held the site last year. Standing on his pile of stones, he calls repeatedly, with bill pointing to the sky

and flippers extended, a signal that means "I have a nest site, and I am looking for a mate." This display attracts females, and nearly always the male is joined within a few days by a female; often she is his mate of the previous year. The female is slightly smaller than the male but otherwise similar in appearance. These two owners defend the nest site against other penguins that may try to take it over.

Male Gentoo displaying; (below) Gentoos nesting on a South Georgia beach.

The colonies are noisy, filled with the crowing and cackling calls of courtship. Rivals for nest sites fight fiercely, pecking and grasping each other with razor-sharp bills, and beating with their hard flippers. Nest sites often change ownership several times during these early days, and partnerships break up and re-form. But by early November most of the birds are paired, and most pairs have a nest site among the tussock grass.

Paired birds bow repeatedly and croon to each other, taking turns to bring nesting material to the site. One sits on the nest and builds, while the other

brings pebbles from the beach, twigs, and pieces of grass or moss which they dig with their bill from grassy banks nearby. Most nests are about half a meter across, with a bowl in the middle just big enough for the bird to sit in comfortably. Some nests, made by young birds breeding for the first time, are no more than a few pebbles and wisps of tussock grass. Others are huge, untidy mounds, so deep and soft that the birds lose their eggs in them.

The partners mate several times between bouts of building. In mating, the male balances on the back of the female, steadying himself with flippers and bill. Like other birds, the male and female penguins have only a single external opening just under the tail, called the cloaca or vent, through which pass waste materials from the body, and also the sperm and eggs. The male presses his tail down under the female's to transfer sperm from his cloaca into hers. The sperm travel up the passage called the oviduct, and fertilize the eggs inside the female. She can now lay fertile eggs.

The first egg, round and bluish white, appears during the second week of November. A second egg is usually laid two or three days after the first. By the end of the month, nearly every pair has two eggs in the nest. The eggs must be kept warm, or incubated, so that they will develop and hatch. The partners share incubation, taking turns of two to four days on the nest and spending their free time

Half-grown Gentoo chicks. ▷

at sea. Usually the male takes the first watch after the eggs are laid. On warm days, the incubating birds stand or crouch over their eggs, stretching occasionally, pecking at passersby, and leaning out to rearrange the nesting material. On cold days they lie on the nest, facing into the wind with flippers tucked firmly by their sides. Through pelting rain, snow storms and blizzards they sit patiently guarding the eggs, shuffling and turning them from time to time and keeping them warm.

When the females return from the sea, they run up the beach and thread their way quickly through the colonies, eager to find their home nest and begin incubating. The sitting bird, broody and comfortable, greets his partner with crooning calls, but often seems content to stay where he is. Eventually, after some gentle pushing and coaxing, he steps down from the nest and his partner takes over. Once he has lost direct contact with the eggs, he quickly becomes alert again. He makes his way down to the shore, joins a group of penguins on the beach, and leaves for the fishing grounds in the morning.

Incubation takes 36 to 38 days, and the two chicks in a nest hatch within a day of each other. Although the chicks are wet on first hatching, the silky gray down that covers them soon dries out, and its fluffiness helps them to keep warm. At first, the chicks are likely to chill if they are exposed to the cold air for longer than a few moments. But their tiny wriggling movements stimulate the brooding bird to huddle closely over them, and keep them warm all the time.

Skuas are a great danger to chicks at this time. Brown Skuas are gull-like birds that feed on penguin eggs and chicks. Every colony of Gentoos is watched over by a pair of skuas, which have their own nest close by. Although they catch some of their

Gentoos on guard against the attack of a Brown Skua.

food at sea, skuas constantly watch the penguin colonies for abandoned eggs or chicks. Penguin parents that leave their nest, even for a minute, may return to find their brood missing, and the two skuas feeding on their eggs or chicks near by.

The piping calls of the chicks, which start even before they hatch, stimulate the parents to feed them. The parent has partly digested food stored in a stomach-like sac called the crop. He regurgitates, or brings up, the food into the back of his throat and offers it to the chicks in the tip of his bill. The chicks are just strong enough to raise their heads and take this first meal. As they grow bigger, their

Gentoo chicks losing the last of their down, and almost ready for the sea.

feeding calls grow louder and more frequent, and the ever-hungry chicks plunge their heads right inside the parent's bill for their food.

By mid-January the chicks, which are now half-grown and rapidly increasing in weight, stray from the nests and gather in nursery groups called crèches. This allows the two parents to leave the colony at the same time, increasing the time they can spend hunting, and the amount of food they can bring home. The chicks crowd closely together. With little to do but keep warm and wait for their next meal, they preen their own down and each other's, and quarrel constantly among themselves. The skuas, with chicks of their own to feed, lurk around the crèches in the hope of a meal. But by

26

this time, strong, well-fed penguin chicks are a match for the skuas and remain safe as long as they stay together. Also there are usually a few dozen adults standing around the crèche; they help to drive off any skuas that come too close.

Parents returning from sea with food in their crop feed only their own chicks. Standing by the side of the crèche, they give a long, crowing call, and their chicks rush out from the group, whistling their noisy feeding calls with great excitement. The parents recognize their own chicks by sound, if not always by sight. Sometimes other hungry chicks rush out too, perhaps mistaking the adult for one

Gentoo parent feeding its chick. The Sheathbill (in the background) scavenges on the colony, picking up fragments of food that the feeding birds drop.

of their own parents. But their whistles are not the right ones, and they are more likely to be pecked than fed. Now over a month old, the chicks are each eating up to a kilogram of food per day—about a quarter of their own weight—and the parents spend nearly all of their time fishing, without a moment's rest between trips.

Gentoo with a half-swallowed fish.

When the chicks are about six to eight weeks old, they begin to shed their gray woolly down and the sleek new feathers of their juvenile plumage appear beneath. By the end of January the first chicks cross the beach in small groups and plunge into the sea. Although slightly smaller than their parents and much thinner, they are perfectly formed little penguins, able to swim and dive at the first attempt.

By this time, most of the adults too have begun to lose their plumage in their yearly moult. Like clothes, feathers wear out and need to be replaced, and penguins cannot swim while they are moulting; so they must fatten up beforehand, laying in enough reserves of blubber to last them three or four weeks. Weighing one and a half times their normal weight, they waddle ashore and find a sheltered corner of the beach or tussock meadow. Soon they seem to swell up, as the new feathers growing underneath push the old feathers out of the way. The old feathers fall out, and for three to four weeks the penguins look tattered and scruffy, and are unable to swim or feed. They stay in sheltered corners, keeping out of the wind and rain, until their new feathers have grown.

Gentoos preening; oiling and arranging
the feathers take up much of
their leisure time.

At this time of the year South Georgia seems to be littered with a snow storm of feathers from millions of moulting penguins. There are about eleven feathers to every square cm of penguin skin. Each of the main body feathers, over 2 cm long, is slightly curved and springy, so that together they form a dense mat with overlapping tips. From the base of each feather grows a little tuft of down, which joins with the one next to it to make a warm undervest close to the skin. Penguins spend a lot of their spare time preening—keeping their feathers in order and slightly greasy, so that they remain waterproof. The waterproofing is so effective that their underlying skin remains completely dry even after several days or weeks at sea.

When the penguins have grown their new plumage, they make their way down to the beaches and return to the sea. Most of the juveniles and adults leave the breeding areas in March and April. They spend the winter at sea, returning occasionally to the frozen, snow-covered beaches of the island.

Macaroni and Chinstrap Penguins, which are slightly smaller than Gentoos (though much more noisy and quarrelsome with each other), have a very similar breeding cycle. As part of their colorful courtship display, Macaroni Penguins shake and wave the vivid golden crests that hang down over their eyes. Each female Macaroni lays two eggs, one bigger than the other, in a nest of pebbles and

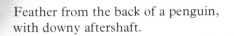

Feather from the back of a penguin,
with downy aftershaft.

Macaroni Penguins of South Georgia.

moss on the steep, rocky slopes of their cliff colony.
Usually they lose the smaller egg early in incubation
and rear only a single chick. Chinstrap Penguins,
which take their name from the helmet-like markings
on their heads, breed much like Gentoos. They
usually manage to rear two chicks when food is
plentiful and the weather mild.

A King Penguin stands about 80 centimeters tall
and weighs about 16 kg—almost three times the
weight of a Gentoo. Because of their greater size,
King Penguins take longer to raise their chicks.
Their eggs take about 54 days to incubate, and their

chicks take even longer to grow and reach independence. So they have adopted a strange breeding cycle that helps them to cope with the long winter. Courtship starts in October, when male King Penguins can be seen displaying to attract unmated females. After calling and shaking his head, the male thrusts out his chest and walks forward, turning his head from side to side in what is called the "advertisement walk." If the female accepts, she follows him. They mate in the same way as other penguins.

The first eggs are laid early in November. There

are no nests or territories; instead, the incubating bird stands with the single, large egg on top of its feet. The egg is tucked under a loose fold of feathered skin from the parent's belly, which keeps it warm. The parents take turns incubating the egg. The first chicks hatch in December.

The chicks have not reached full size by winter, and so they remain in the colony throughout the winter, huddled together in enormous crèches. They are visited by the parents and fed at irregular intervals—sometimes only every third or fourth week. All the chicks lose weight and many of the smaller ones die of starvation during the coldest months of the winter—June, July and August. In September, food becomes more plentiful and the parents feed their chicks more often. By October and November the surviving chicks are moulting and leaving for the sea. The first eggs of the new season—mostly laid by birds that lost their chicks early in the previous winter—are already on the way. Parents that have succeeded in raising chicks lay later, in January or February. With luck, they may manage to raise their chick to a good weight—and a fair chance of survival—before winter comes upon them again. Because the breeding cycle takes over a year to complete, King Penguins may raise two chicks in three years, although many will probably be successful only once every two years.

33

◁King Penguins incubating (left, center) and holding a month-old chick (right).

4

Penguins of the Antarctic

Penguins are most plentiful and varied on the cool-temperate islands of the southern ocean. But farther south, on the polar continent itself, live the true Antarctic penguins—the Adelies, which are related to Gentoos, and the Emperors, which are the large polar cousins of the King Penguins. In this intensely cold climate, winter temperatures can fall as low as $-50°C$, and the summer temperatures seldom

Courtship display of
Adelie Penguins.

rise above freezing point. The sea is frozen for ten months of the year or more, and the land is a desert—so cold and dry that even mosses and lichens have difficulty in growing.

Keeping warm is not difficult for birds that are well fed and have a good overcoat of feathers, as the polar penguins do. Their main problem is to arrange their breeding cycle so that the chicks are ready to go to sea just before the end of the very short summer. This gives both parents and chicks the time they need to grow thick plumage and build up their stores of body fat before winter sets in.

Adelie Penguins start breeding in October, when the air temperature may still be as low as $-30°C$ and the sea is frozen for many kilometers around the colonies. One of the first signs of spring in Antarctica is to see the Adelies streaming in file across the sea ice, scrambling among the rough patches on their short stumpy legs, and tobogganing over the smoother areas on their shining breast feathers.

Adelies tobogganing; feet and flippers propel them over the hard-packed snow.

Finding their nest site of the previous year on the wind-swept rookeries, they court, rebuild their pebble nests, mate and lay two eggs, all in two or three weeks of feverish activity. Because of the sea ice, which may still extend 50 to 60 kilometers out from the continent itself, they cannot go to the sea for a quick meal. Females return to the sea to feed as soon as their eggs are laid, often having

Adelies diving into a calm sea.

fasted for three weeks or more. Males stay at the nest site to incubate the eggs and may go as long as five or six weeks without food.

By November and December the sea ice has usually broken up, and in January most of the chicks grow and fatten rapidly. They moult from their silver-gray down into juvenile plumage long before they are fully grown. Young Adelies become independent sooner than the young of most other species, giving their parents time to complete their own post-breeding moult and fatten again before the short summer is over.

Emperor Penguins are the biggest of all penguins, growing up to 110 cm tall and weighing 30 kg or more. Like King Penguins, they take longer than other species to incubate their eggs and rear their chicks. To have the chicks ready for the sea in summer, Emperors must mate in autumn and incubate their eggs through the depths of the polar winter. They gather on inshore sea ice, which is warmer than the land in winter. After an elaborate courtship, they usually mate with their partner from the previous year and lay their eggs in late May and June. Like King Penguins, Emperors do not make nests; instead the males alone incubate the single egg on their feet, covered by a fold of skin, for two months. These are the two coldest and darkest months of winter, with temperatures seldom rising above $-20°C$ and constant biting winds. To keep

Male Emperor Penguins incubating. The single egg
rests on the feet, under a warm fold of feathered skin.

warm the incubating males pack closely together,
sometimes several hundred of them in a single
group. Through the long, cold weeks they do not
eat, but live on their reserves of fat. The incubating
birds grow very thin, sometimes losing half their
body weight.

The females spend their winter at the ice edge,
feeding at the sea, and return to the colonies just as
the chicks are hatching out. The females relieve

the males and guard the chicks on their feet while the males journey to the sea to fatten up. The food the females bring in their crops is regurgitated and fed to the chicks for the first two or three weeks. Then the two parents take turns going to the sea to catch food, and later they both hunt while the chicks stand huddled in crèches, waiting for their return. By midsummer the chicks are half as big as their parents, and many have already moulted into juvenile plumage. The chicks become independent at a time when sea ice is breaking and food is plentiful. Often the sea ice beneath them breaks into floes, and all that remains of the colony floats safely off northwards to the open sea.

Emperor Penguins with two-month-old chicks.

5

Penguins of warmer climates

Just as polar penguins are well adapted for the life which they lead, so tropical and subtropical species have similar kinds of adaptations for their rather different life styles. Penguins of warm climates are slimmer than polar species; their plumage is thinner and they have no need for the huge reserves of fat that penguins of cold climates carry with them. Most live underground in caves or burrows, or in thick forests near the sea that protect them from the heat of the sun. Many are active on land only at night, when the air is cool and there are fewer predators—gulls, skuas, dogs or people—awake to harm them.

Four species of penguins from temperate and tropical coasts—Magellanic, Peruvian, Jackass and Galapagos.

Typical of the warmer climate species are the Magellanic Penguins of South America. In the wet forests of southern Chile they burrow among the roots of trees near the sea. On the drier eastern shores of Argentina they burrow in sandy soils, forming huge underground cities of tens or hundreds of thousands of nests. The mournful braying and wailing of the penguins, emerging from holes in the ground, has given rise to legends of ghosts and devils along the fog-ridden coast of Patagonia. Peruvian Penguins, closely related to the Magellanic Penguins but smaller, nest in similar situations on the off-shore islands of Peru. On the Galapagos Islands, which straddle the Equator west of South America, Galapagos Penguins nest in caves close to the sea. Currents of cool water from the south help to lessen the extreme heat, and make it possible for them to live in a tropical climate. Another species

of burrowing penguin, the little Jackass or Black-footed Penguin, lives on islands off the south-western tip of South Africa, again in a place where cold currents help to chill both the sea and the air.

Snares Island Penguins (left) live on one tiny group of islands south of New Zealand. Fiordland Penguins (right) nest among coastal forests of New Zealand's South Island.

The crested penguins of New Zealand—the Fiordland and Snares Island Penguins—live mainly in wet coastal forests. They make their nests of sticks and grass, nestled among rocks or tree roots or in mounds of mud. There are usually two eggs but only one survives in each nest. The rookeries are noisy and very smelly. One of the few places in the world where penguins perch in trees is on the Snares Islands. They often scramble onto the lower branches, which are drier and more comfortable than the muddy ground below.

Little Blue or Fairy Penguins of New Zealand and Australia live in crevices or caverns along the rocky shores, and in burrows among sand dunes. They are surprisingly small; it would take 30 of them to outweigh a single Emperor. Usually several dozen pairs nest together in the same area. They hide during the hot sunny days, but emerge and wander in the evenings. Near Melbourne, in south Australia, the evening march of Little Blue Penguins across the beach is a tourist attraction, but their numbers have been reduced by cats, dogs and other enemies, and by the destruction of their habitat.

Fairy or Little Blue Penguins of southern Australia and New Zealand—a species which nests in caves and burrows.

6

Enemies

Penguins have many natural enemies both on land and at sea. On land, the main enemies are the skuas that watch over the rookeries, snatching eggs and unguarded chicks.

At sea, adults and young penguins are attacked by seals and by large seabirds called Giant Petrels. Leopard Seals—long, lithe creatures with formidable teeth—lurk in the sea near colonies, waiting to seize unsuspecting penguins. They pursue penguins under water with great agility and speed. Fur Seals, too, chase penguins in the water, and may even follow them through the surf and chase them across the beaches. Giant Petrels float off shore,

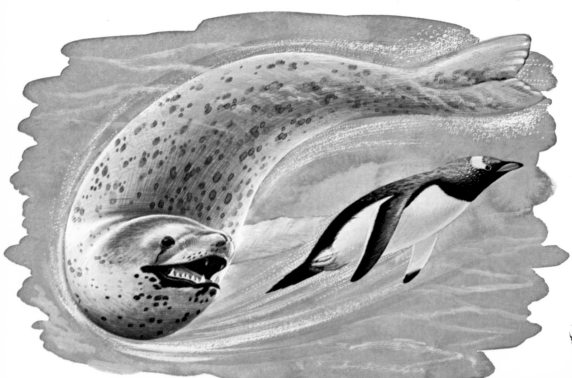

especially at the end of summer, when the beaches are crowded with young birds entering the water for the first time. Although able to swim, these newly fledged juveniles are slower and less agile than adults, and often fall prey to the sharp, heavy bills of the Petrels. Sharks and Killer Whales have also been known to hunt penguins.

Giant Petrels sometimes attack young penguins during their first swim.

Penguins are very cautious when entering the sea. Often they parade up and down along the beach for a long time before approaching the water's edge. They line up on the shores in big groups, scanning the sea for signs of a Leopard Seal. As more penguins jostle at the back, the ones in front get pushed into the water, and then they all dive in.

Like most other seabirds, penguins of warmer climates are suffering from the activities and the spread of people. The greatest hazard is oil, which

◁ Leopard Seal—one of the few enemies of penguins at sea.

leaks from tankers and other ships, and pollutes the surface of the sea. Penguins that get oil on their feathers cannot preen it off. They are either poisoned by it, or starve to death because the oil prevents them from swimming and diving properly. In more inhabited coastal areas development of roads, railways and housing estates cuts many penguins off from their traditional breeding grounds. Countries like New Zealand, Australia and South Africa, which are the home of penguins, have made laws that help to protect them. But despite this, several species are decreasing in numbers, and are no longer found in areas where they were once plentiful. Penguins of the colder regions fare better, because there is less pollution and there are fewer people to interfere with them, or with the places they live in.

Inquisitive Magellanic Penguin.

Index